P9-CRB-081

# FELONY PROSECUTION

## YOUR LEGAL RIGHTS

PETE SCHAUER

# ROSEN
## PUBLISHING

New York

Published in 2015 by The Rosen Publishing Group, Inc.
29 East 21st Street, New York, NY 10010

First Edition

**Expert Reviewer:** Lindsay A. Lewis, Esq.

**Library of Congress Cataloging-in-Publication Data**

Schauer, Peter J., author.
Felony prosecution: your legal rights / Pete Schauer.
    pages cm.—(Know your rights)
Includes bibliographical references and index.
ISBN 978-1-4777-8024-4 (library bound) —
ISBN 978-1-4777-8025-1 (pbk.) — ISBN 978-1-4777-8026-8
(6-pack)
1. Violent crimes—United States—Juvenile literature. 2. Offenses against the person—United States—Juvenile literature. 3. Criminal procedure—United States—Juvenile literature. 4. Juvenile justice, Administration of—United States—Juvenile literature. I. Title.
KF9304.S33 2014
345.73'025—dc23

2014009317

*Manufactured in the United States of America*

# CONTENTS

# INTRODUCTION

D id you know that the decisions you make as a juvenile can potentially affect the rest of your life? Many young adults get caught up with a crowd that may engage in illegal activities. Sometimes this results in nothing more than a wild youth. Other times, however, individuals are taken down a bad path that affects their entire lives. On the bright side, research of late has proven that juvenile crime and felonies are down across the board. According to the Office of Juvenile Justice and Delinquency Prevention (OJJDP), the juvenile arrest rate for all offenses declined 48 percent in 2011 from 1996, when the rate was at its highest in the twenty years prior. Further research from the OJJDP shows that the overall juvenile arrest rate dropped 32 percent in 2011 from its rate in 1980.

While this is certainly encouraging news for both juveniles and their parents, it's still extremely important for young adults to understand juvenile felony prosecution and how to avoid it altogether. And although the rates are dropping, there are still far too many juveniles being accused and prosecuted for felonies.

One instance is a case in Florida where a thirteen-year-old boy was arrested for carrying a loaded gun onto a school bus. Although the boy didn't commit a violent act, he was charged with multiple felonies—including carrying a concealed firearm—because of a poor decision he made at a young age. Regardless of where he got the gun or what his reasons were for carrying it, he'll now have to go

*A young boy is fingerprinted at the police station after being arrested.*

through the Department of Juvenile Justice facility to find out what the future holds for him.

While it's true that juveniles are typically treated differently than adults when it comes to prosecution, that's not always the case. There are times when juveniles are treated as adults because of the heinousness of the crime, among other factors.

Felony convictions are treated with severe legal recourse. While punishment is often a prison sentence, there are a number of alternative penalties and punishments that a judge can enforce. One thing judges can't do is sentence a juvenile to life in prison without parole. Although draconian punishment is still an issue in both state and federal court, the Supreme Court ruled that juveniles couldn't be sentenced to life without parole on the basis that it constitutes cruel and unusual punishment.

With that said, committing a felony at a young age is a serious matter and can set a young adult back in multiple ways, including personal relationships, education, career path, and more. With the right amount of help and guidance from a multitude of people, though, it is possible to recover from a felony.

One of the best things you can do is understand the law and learn about what constitutes a felony so that you can avoid it at all costs and continue down the right path. This volume will teach you the ins and outs of juvenile felonies, teaching you what they are, how they are tried in court, and how they can affect your life. Should you find yourself in a situation that constitutes a felony charge, use this volume as a guide throughout the procedures.

# CHAPTER 1

# WHAT ARE VIOLENT CRIMES AND FELONIES?

Crime and violence are often depicted in movies, video games, and television shows, giving young and impressionable teenagers the wrong idea about what it means to grow up. Upon hearing the term, you'd think that a violent crime would mean physically harming someone, but that's not necessarily correct. Even the threat of hurting an individual can be classified as a violent crime.

According to the Federal Bureau of Investigation's (FBI) official website, a violent crime is considered any offense that involves force or the threat of force. Something that a lot of people don't realize is that there doesn't have to be physical contact in order for something to be ruled a violent crime. Additionally, some crimes are inherently violent without the actual use of physical force, such as certain terrorism threats. It's important to note that the ruling on whether a crime was violent or not can largely affect both the penalties handed down by a judge as well as conditions of imprisonment and eligibility for certain programs, such as drug rehabilitation facilities.

A violent crime falls under the category of a felony. A felony is more serious in degree than a misdemeanor. Punishment for felonies can consist of a prison sentence in a state or federal prison, or worse, the death sentence.

Not all violent felonies result in imprisonment, as probation is an appropriate punishment, but that doesn't change the fact that committing a felony is a serious matter. A felony differs from a misdemeanor because misdemeanors are punishable only by a fine and/or up to one year's worth of time spent in a county jail.

It's important to know that the federal and state laws differ when it comes to violent felonies. Federal crimes violate federal laws while state crimes break state laws. Each state has its own laws and constitutions, but it is possible for a crime to fall under both the state and federal law. Prosecution depends on the state the crime was committed in.

While certain violent felonies, like murder and rape, are more vicious than others, there are many acts of violence that fall under the umbrella of violent felonies. Let's learn about the four main forms of violent felonies and examples of each.

# MURDER AND VOLUNTARY MANSLAUGHTER

The act of murder is something our society is unfortunately very familiar with. As evidenced by highly publicized murder trials, such as the O. J. Simpson trial in 1995 and 2011's trial of Casey Anthony, murder has consistently been in the spotlight in the United States and in countries all over the world. Murder is the most heinous violent felony of the four categories, as it involves the unlawful killing of a human.

*O. J. Simpson appears in a Los Angeles court in 1995 after being accused of murdering his ex-wife, Nicole Brown, and Ronald Goldman, a restaurant waiter.*

Murder is distinguished by degree. Although definitions vary by state, first-degree murder involves pre-meditation. In other words, a person plots or plans on taking the life of another human being. Voluntary manslaughter is the act of killing a person without planning it, or killing "in the act of passion." An example of voluntary manslaughter would be getting into an argument with someone and killing him, having not planned on killing him prior to the argument.

Committing the act of murder or manslaughter comes with serious and harsh consequences, an average of twenty years behind bars. No matter what another person did to you, it's never worth throwing away your life to end someone else's. There are many ways to solve a problem or an issue with another individual, and killing him certainly isn't the answer and won't solve your problems. The best thing you can do is to try to talk to the person to solve the issue at hand, and if that doesn't work, find other nonviolent ways to resolve the problem, such as counseling.

## FORCIBLE RAPE AND SEXUAL ASSAULT

Often depicted in television shows like *Law and Order: Special Victims Unit*, rape is another serious violent felony. Rape is a sexual offense against another person in which the individual doesn't give consent for sexual contact. Force is used in some, but not all, cases of rape. Some victims are unable to consent to sexual intercourse because they are physically or mentally disabled or incapacitated; impaired by substances, such as drugs and alcohol; or minors. In the United States, the age of consent varies by jurisdiction, but all states set their limits between the age of sixteen and eighteen.

One of the most famous rape cases in the United States was the 2012 Steubenville High School case, in which a group of male students sexually assaulted a sixteen-year-old girl who was impaired by alcohol. Two boys were charged in the case, in which videos and text messages of the sexual acts were used as evidence, making it easy for the Ohio jury to convict the two teenagers.

## FELONY STATISTICS

In 2012, violent crime increased 0.7 percent from the previous year, with an estimated 14,827 murders, 84,376 forcible rapes, 354,520 robberies, and 760,739 aggravated assaults reported to law enforcement, according to the FBI.

During the teenage years when high school students start experimenting with alcohol and drugs, impaired teens sometimes take advantage of others who are incapacitated, which is defined as rape. This is something that should be taken extremely seriously by teenagers. The law states that it is never permissible to have sexual relations with another person unless he or she gives you consent.

# ROBBERY

In video games like *Grand Theft Auto*, a felony like robbery is glorified, but in the real world, being convicted of robbery is no joke. By definition, robbery is the use, or the threat of use, of force to take something that belongs to another individual. Robbery is often confused with other crimes like burglary and shoplifting, but there is one key difference—violence. Robbery requires the use or intent to use violence. For example, if you go into a stranger's house and steal something, that's considered burglary. If you enter a stranger's home and steal her

*This surveillance footage shows an armed robbery taking place at Merchants Bank in Colchester, Vermont.*

belongings while holding her at gunpoint, then that is considered robbery.

Stealing from another person is never condoned, and the legal system will penalize you for it. If you don't have the money to purchase something that you want, it's a lot more gratifying to work toward something and then purchase it down the road rather than to steal it. Sometimes, individuals who go down the wrong path and abuse drugs feel forced to rob others to support their drug habit, but that's certainly not the answer. If you have a drug problem, the smartest thing to do is to seek help from an established rehabilitation facility. While there are various reasons why people commit the felony of robbery, the easiest thing to do is to avoid it altogether and work hard for everything in life.

## AGGRAVATED ASSAULT

Aggravated assault is a bit trickier than the other three violent felonies because there are different levels and types of assault. There's assault, in which an individual can be charged for physically injuring someone or even conveying the idea that he's going to inflict physical harm on a person. Then there's aggravated assault, which is considered a felony that involves an assault committed with a weapon or the intent to commit a heinous crime like rape or murder. An example of assault would be attacking a fellow student at school and using physical harm against him. That charge would increase to an aggravated assault charge if a weapon like a gun or knife were used in the attack.

## GANG ASSOCIATION

Violent felonies such as aggravated assault, murder, robbery, and rape are often associated with gangs, which can be extremely impressionable on young teens, especially in certain neighborhoods across the United States. Gang violence is something that is not to be taken lightly. In 2011, the National Gang Threat Assessment report found that gangs are responsible for an average of 48

*Violent crimes and felonies are frequently connected to gangs, whose members target impressionable teens for recruitment.*

percent of violent crime in most jurisdictions, going all the way up to 90 percent in other jurisdictions.

Even for the common teenager not affiliated with a gang, middle school and high school students solve their problems with their fists at times, which is a big mistake. Regardless of what the charge is considered, you don't want to be accused of any type of assault. Fights in school and on the streets aren't necessarily uncommon, but what a lot of teens don't realize is that they can be charged for a crime for getting into a fistfight.

According to the National Institute of Justice, there were 225 arrests for Violent Crime Index offenses for every 100,000 juveniles between the age of ten and seventeen in 2010. While the juvenile arrest rate has fallen 55 percent from 1994, there are still too many violent felonies being committed by today's youth. If there's one thing that should be taken from this chapter, it's that violent crimes come in many different forms and come with harsh penalties that can be devastating to a young person's life. Now that you know what's considered a felony, you can be more careful of your actions.

# CHAPTER 2

# WHAT TO DO IF YOU'RE ARRESTED

Navigating the legal process is not easy. In the event that you're ever accused of committing a felony, you should know that you have rights. Just because you were accused of, or even arrested for, a felony, doesn't automatically mean that you're going to prison and that your life is ruined. There are many instances in which people are questioned by the police for crimes that they didn't commit. When approached by a police officer or another member of law enforcement, you should inquire as to whether you're under arrest and make it known that you want a lawyer. You should not answer any questions without a lawyer present. If you did commit the crime, there are many factors that must be taken into consideration, with the most important being legal representation.

## GETTING LEGAL REPRESENTATION

Seeking legal representation is the single most important thing you will do if you are being accused of committing a felony. Since your attorney will primarily be the one representing your innocence in court, it's important that you take your time and decide upon a lawyer that both you and your family feel comfortable with. It's well known that lawyer fees aren't cheap, but when your life depends on their skills and expertise in the courtroom, you have to decide if the cost of an attorney outweighs the possibility of being convicted for a crime and spending time in jail.

In the U.S. legal system, if you can't afford the cost of an attorney for a felony case, the court will appoint one for you. These court-appointed lawyers are typically legal aids and public defenders. While they usually are burdened

*A young teen sits with her attorney in court.*

with a large caseload, the lawyers appointed by the court system are typically extremely familiar with the law, since they spend most of their time in the courtroom. Additionally, with the knowledge gained from this book, you'll be armed with the necessary tools and questions to assure that you're being well represented in court.

If you can afford an attorney, it's recommended that you consult with him or her before speaking to a member of law enforcement so as not to implicate yourself further. As far as the cost of hiring a criminal defense attorney, there are a number of things that factor into the price, including location, experience, and the complexity of the case. When it comes to billing, there are usually two main options: hourly billing or case billing. It would be wise to ask your attorney what the most cost-effective route is, and if it's possible to work on a retainer against the amount of money that is spent. Cases are often billed in sections, for the pre-trial and then again if the case does go to trial. State cases have a higher chance of going to trial, but federal cases rarely do. In a state case, a plea is often the most cost-effective way to resolve a case because it can result in lesser penalties and allows for negotiation.

To receive adequate advice and legal representation, it's important to do research. When conducting your research, you should be looking for reliable websites, such as state bar sites, that rate lawyers and inform you of any negative infractions or disciplinary violations against the lawyer. One way to find legal representation is by asking friends and family if they know of a reliable attorney. It's recommended that you hire an attorney who has experience representing other clients for the same types of crimes, as his familiarity with the crime and case will be beneficial to you throughout the process. When you meet with your lawyer, you should ask as many questions as possible. He is the one working for you, so you need to be comfortable and confident that he'll represent you to the best of his ability in court.

# UNDERSTANDING THE LEGAL PROCESS

The legal process isn't easy to learn or understand. There are numerous factors that go into deciding if a person is guilty and, if so, what type of penalty will be handed down. The legal process begins immediately upon arrest when the arresting officer reads you your Miranda rights, which consist of the following: you have the right to remain silent, the right to legal counsel, and the right to be told that anything you say can be used in a court of law against you. If a police officer fails to read you your Miranda rights, the prosecutor can't use anything that you say during the arrest as evidence at trial.

Upon being arrested for a felony or crime, an arraignment will be held. The arraignment is your first appearance before a judge where you are initially charged with a complaint. The main purpose of the arraignment for a felony case is to establish whether there are any conditions that permit your release, such as bail. Should the case require it, the next step is either a preliminary hearing or a case before the grand jury. Whether a preliminary hearing is

Three teens appear in court for their arraignment on first-degree murder charges. The teens were accused of beating a homeless man to death.

scheduled or a case before the grand jury is held is determined by the state. The purpose of the preliminary hearing is to determine if there is probable cause for you to be indicted, or formally charged with a felony.

Preliminary hearings are held at the lowest level of local court, but are only necessary if the prosecutor has filed the charge without asking the grand jury for an official indictment. Preliminary hearings are usually held within a few days after the arraignment. So as not to show the defense its strategy, the prosecution will usually only present enough evidence to show the probability of guilt. If the judge believes there's enough evidence to warrant a trial, the case will be sent to the grand jury. If the judge doesn't feel that the evidence is strong enough, the charges will be dropped and the case is dismissed.

When the case moves to the grand jury level, it's up to the grand jury to decide if you'll be indicted for the crime that you've been accused of committing. To do so, the grand jury meets in secret and uses evidence such as documents and sworn testimonies and depositions, from witnesses called upon by the prosecution, to make its decision. As the defendant, you're also eligible to take the stand and testify on your own behalf before the grand jury, but it's important that you consult with your lawyer about the decision to testify. A grand jury can't decide if you're guilty of the crime, but only if there's enough evidence to file a charge against you. If there's enough evidence to believe that you committed the crime, the grand jury will indict you and send the case to trial. If the jury fails to indict the defendant, the case is dismissed. That's not to say that charges can be brought against the defendant again, but prosecutors usually only present a case to the grand jury if they feel confident they will get an indictment.

If the grand jury decides to indict you, then you will be brought to court to be arraigned on the indictment. You will now enter a plea of either guilty or not guilty. If you plead not guilty, then your case will move to trial. In the meantime, your lawyer may try various tactics to weaken the prosecution's case and either negotiate with the prosecution or get your case dismissed.

While this is just the beginning of the legal process for you, it's easy to see why hiring an experienced lawyer is important. Your lawyer will be representing you and will be defending you against the prosecution, which is entitled to call witnesses to the stand for questioning.

The next step in the process is the trial, where your lawyer will attempt to prove your innocence before a judge and jury. The importance of legal representation is at its highest during the trial since your attorney will primarily

*A judge presides over a trial in session in the courtroom.*

be your voice throughout the length of the trial. A lot will be said, but in order for a person to be indicted, the prosecution must present the judge and jury with legal evidence, or proof that the person on trial committed the crime beyond reasonable doubt.

When the trial concludes, the jury will either find the defendant guilty or not guilty. If you're found guilty of a felony, the judge will sentence you to a punishment, which could range anywhere from community service to incarceration. Your lawyer should argue that the judge show as much leniency as possible when sentencing, depending on your situation. Also, you must be aware that if you are not a U.S. citizen and you plead guilty to a felony, you could face deportation. It is important to alert your attorney to your immigration status immediately, since that can affect his or her strategy.

Depending on a few factors, such as your criminal record and age, it's possible that you could be tried as a juvenile in juvenile court. In terms of outcome, the main difference between juvenile court and regular court is that regular court aims to punish the convicted while juvenile

## THE ROLE OF WITNESSES

Witnesses aren't needed throughout every step of the legal process. Typically, witnesses are asked to attend court only for a preliminary hearing, grand jury hearing, a witness conference, or a trial.

court focuses on rehabilitation and education. The idea of juvenile court is to help the young individual avoid legal trouble down the road. Juveniles are considered anyone under the age of eighteen, but if you commit a serious crime like murder, it's very possible that you would be tried as an adult. It's also possible to be tried as a youthful offender in adult court. This, however, comes with some hesitation, as it can have consequences if you are charged with a crime in the future. For instance, in federal court, a youthful offender conviction could result in a higher criminal history category, leading to potential for a higher sentence. Again, this is why it is important to have an experienced lawyer and to make sure you have honest discussions.

# CHAPTER 3

# CONSEQUENCES AND PENALTIES

Everyone makes mistakes, but when you're young, it's hard to imagine that your actions at such a young age could define your future. Making a bad decision when you are young can result in serious jail time—at the maximum, a lifetime behind bars. The consequences and penalties that come along with a felony conviction are extremely serious and can be detrimental to a juvenile's life.

Not only is a punishment like a prison sentence a possibility, but also the resulting emotional and mental damage can leave juveniles to deal with a lifetime full of mental health issues and regret. Aside from the mental and emotional damage, there are a multitude of punishments that come with being convicted of a felony, all of which are determined by a judge and depend on your plea.

Entering a plea, or stating whether you're pleading guilty or not guilty, plays a huge factor in the type of punishment you'll receive. If you were to plead guilty and admit that you committed the crime, it's likely that you'd receive a reduced punishment in return for the guilty plea. This is usually a tempting deal for both you and your lawyer, as it means avoiding trial and a harsher punishment.

On the other hand, you could receive a much harsher punishment by rejecting a plea bargain and going to trial.

Let's say you were offered a deal where punishment would be one year of electronic monitoring—or house arrest—and you think that penalty is too harsh so you decide to go to trial. If convicted, you could face a much more severe punishment, like multiple years of jail time. The judge and prosecutor often learn more about the crime committed during trial, meaning that there's more time to hear and see the evidence against the defendant. In cases where the evidence is especially incriminating, judges will often hand down a much more severe punishment.

Pleading no contest is also an option, but with this type of plea, you're accepting a sentence for a particular crime but not admitting to the allegations, or not entering a guilty plea. One of the benefits of entering a plea of no contest is that there's no real admission of guilt, which helps so as to not further implicate yourself down the road.

## PROBATION

Being put on probation after being convicted of a felony is one of the most sought-after outcomes of a trial for the defense. Being put on probation allows you to remain at liberty, so long as you follow the conditions of your probation, check in with your probation officer as required, and do not violate the terms of your probation or commit another crime, which could result in the imposition of a prison sentence. Probation is usually only given to first-time offenders or those who haven't committed a serious crime.

There are some restrictions, though. If you violate probation—or get into any sort of legal trouble—you could be sentenced to a much harsher penalty, including time spent in jail. Additionally, being on probation means having regular meetings with your probation officer, who's in charge of making sure you're staying out of trouble. If you serve your probationary term without getting into any trouble, you've then served your punishment and can get back to your regular life. Keep in mind that a judge likely won't be as lenient in the event that you commit another crime.

*An offender meets and checks in with his probation officer.*

# COUNSELING

Some judges require that the convicted individual receive mandatory counseling by a psychologist or a school counselor. The cases in which counseling is assigned as a punishment are usually less serious and are for first-time offenders, like probation is. The hope behind sending a juvenile to counseling is that she can work through her issues with the counselor and understand the mistakes that were made and why, so as not to end up in a similar situation again. Sending a teenager for counseling also keeps him busy and out of trouble that he could potentially be getting into after school. If the individual gets into trouble while going for counseling, the judge can make a decision to inflict further punishment upon him, which will likely come in the form of a harsher penalty.

# ELECTRONIC MONITORING

In exchange for not having to spend time in a juvenile detention facility or a jail, some judges will decide that a convicted felon should be monitored, but not in an official facility. How is that possible? Through electronic monitoring. Also known as house arrest, electronic monitoring is when an individual is required to wear a bracelet on her wrist or ankle so that her location can be monitored at all times. While electronic monitoring is certainly a lenient alternative to being confined to a jail cell, it often means the convicted individual isn't allowed to leave her house, except to go to work, meet with her attorney, or attend

*A teenager entering a county parole facility wears an electronic ankle monitor, which is used to track his whereabouts while he's under house arrest.*

school, for instance. Nonetheless, house arrest is still a more favorable way to serve a punishment handed down by a judge.

# COMMUNITY SERVICE

In exchange for not having to spend time behind bars, some judges hand down a punishment of community service. Community service can range anywhere from picking up trash on the side of the highway to volunteering at a soup kitchen or speaking to an auditorium full of high school students. Either way, the idea is to reform the convicted felon, hoping that he learns his lesson while giving back to the community. A community service sentence is viewed as a slap on the wrist by some, but if the convicted felon didn't commit too serious of a crime, community service is an admissible punishment. Not only is he giving back to the community, but he's hopefully learning from his mistakes.

# JUVENILE DETENTION

If the judge feels that the punishment for a felony warrants a harsher penalty than community service, you could be sent to juvenile detention, which is a type of jail for people under the age of eighteen. Juvenile detention, which is also known as juvenile hall, is designed for short-term stays that attempt to reform and teach the teenager a lesson. There are also secured juvenile facilities, known as camps, which are meant for longer stays, usually because of a more serious crime. Juvenile detention is the closest thing to a

*Offenders sentenced to juvenile detention must attend classes in traditional academic subjects. They also learn coping and other life skills.*

prison sentence for an individual under eighteen and should not be thought of as a light punishment.

## PRISON SENTENCE

For serious felonies and those who have been accused or convicted multiple times, prison sentences are likely. Except for the death penalty, a prison sentence is the harshest punishment that can be handed out for

31

## JUVENILES AND THE DEATH PENALTY

On March 1, 2005, in the *Roper v. Simmons* case, it was ruled that it was unconstitutional for juveniles to be sentenced to death. Prior to that ruling, twenty-two juveniles received the death penalty between 1976 and 2005, according to CNN.

committing a violent felony. While juveniles can't be sentenced to the death penalty, they most definitely can receive a prison sentence. According to the Annie E. Casey Foundation, the rate of juveniles being imprisoned has dropped roughly 40 percent from 1995. Nonetheless, 70,792 juveniles were still being punished in correctional facilities in 2010.

The length of the prison sentence is completely up to the judge, taking into account the severity of the crime and your criminal record. A judge can't hand down an excessive punishment, as it would be considered cruel and unusual punishment.

That's not to say that juveniles can't be sentenced to solitary confinement in a juvenile detention facility, which can be emotionally and physically damaging to teens. According to Amy Fettig and Tanya Greene of the ACLU National Prison Project, more than seventy thousand juveniles spend their days in solitary confinement at juvenile detention facilities, with roughly twenty-one hours per day spent in a small room. The lack of human contact and time spent in a small cell can be extremely harmful to teenagers, which is why it's a somewhat controversial sentence. Juveniles at this age are accustomed

*Juvenile solitary confinement consists of spending twenty-one hours per day alone, locked in a small, empty room.*

to having active social lives and it's a serious eye-opener when they're forced to spend the majority of their days alone. Nonetheless, serious felonies warrant serious punishments, and it takes harsh discipline and rehabilitation to try and avoid another incident.

# ALTERNATIVES TO INCARCERATION PROGRAMS

Sometimes, judges feel that being locked up behind bars isn't the most appropriate or beneficial punishment for an individual, so they'll sentence the convicted felon to a court-mandated program that either serves to reduce a prison sentence or stands in its place. In federal court, there are programs that convicted felons can enroll in once they are incarcerated, such as the Residential Drug Abuse Program (RDAP), which can help to reduce the length of a prison sentence. Additionally, things like New York's SHOCK program can serve in the place of a prison sentence. The SHOCK program is a military-style disciplinary program where young adults can receive substance abuse treatment, academic education, and more help for when they return to their normal lives, according to the National Institute of Justice. There are programs similar to these all over the country, so your best bet is to ask your lawyer about these types of programs and your potential eligibility before researching them.

# CHAPTER 4

# RETURNING TO NORMALCY

Returning to a normal life, especially after serving a prison sentence, isn't easy. Even for convicted felons who avoided prison time but were punished through actions like electronic monitoring, returning to normalcy is something that takes time. Furthermore, committing a felony and serving time for it behind prison bars can affect a person on many different levels, including in his personal relationships, career opportunities, emotional health, and much more. Just adjusting to everyday life—something as simple as being able to wake up in your own bed and prepare breakfast for yourself—can take some getting used to.

Just because you're no longer in prison or serving a punishment doesn't mean that you return to the ordinary life that you had before you committed the crime. Whether you're trying to get back in school or are looking for a job, there are certain things you need to know in order to accomplish your end goal of returning to normalcy.

## REENTERING SCHOOL

Education is one of the most important things in a teenager's life. You may not believe it while you're young, but what you learn in school, especially at the middle and high school level, is what's going to help you succeed in life. Since most jobs require a high school degree or the passing of a GED (General Education Development) test, it's clear that a proper education is the key to a successful

*Returning to your regular life after serving punishment for a felony can be a difficult adjustment. You may find that your friends are not supportive of your attempts to start fresh.*

life. According to the Federal Reserve Bank of St. Louis, in September 2013, the unemployment rate for individuals without a high school diploma was 10.3 percent, which was more than 3 percent higher than the national rate at the time. Without a formal education, it's difficult to get a job, and without income, it's nearly impossible to survive, making school and education all the more important.

After serving a punishment for a felony, it's important that you align yourself with the right people who will help you get back in school and on the right path, whether it be your family, friends, or a counselor. Additionally, there are nonprofit organizations, such as the Children's Defense Fund (CDF), whose main goal is to help juveniles who have been convicted of a crime get back on their feet. According to the CDF, 48 percent of individuals in the juvenile justice system are functioning below the grade level that's appropriate for their age, which further highlights the importance of an education to advancement in one's career. Returning to school after being punished for a felony isn't easy, but with the right help and support, you can get back on your feet and start to feel like a normal student once again.

## GETTING A JOB

Even after serving a punishment for committing a felony, there are still boundaries that need to be overcome in order to return to a normal life. One of those boundaries comes in the form of finding a job.

Working is one of the best things a juvenile who has recently been convicted of a crime can do, as it keeps her out of trouble and provides her with an income at the same time. But it can be difficult to find a job with a criminal record. Most applications ask whether you've ever been convicted of a crime, and if you answer yes, the chance of you getting a job significantly drops.

Although companies aren't supposed to discriminate against those who have been convicted of a crime, the reality is that some companies do. To combat that, according to the Washington Informer, politicians are trying to ban employers from being allowed to ask about a person's criminal background on the initial employment inquiry form, saving that question for after the initial inquiry has been passed and employment is being offered.

First, it is important to discuss your education and career goals with your lawyer prior to the resolution of your case. She can advise you on how best to proceed in order to pursue your goals, such as getting a job. If you wish to enter the military or work in law enforcement or for any government agency, the fact of a prior conviction can ruin your chances. It can also prevent you from holding public office and can have other consequences in terms of the type of career you will be able to pursue. In some cases, however, a lawyer can help you avoid these consequences.

In the meantime, there are several organizations that focus on helping ex-convicts find employment. For example, Yale University's Urban Resources Initiative trains indivduals for and places them in careers in forestry and horticulture, while the Center for Employment

*An ex-convict works at a warehouse. Large corporations are beginning to remove criminal questions from applications while the government continues to pass laws that will help convicted felons obtain employment.*

Opportunities in New York helps ex-felons obtain work. There are places and organizations all over the country that help ex-felons get jobs. If you need help finding a job after being convicted of a crime, search the Internet and look for an established and reliable organization that can help you start or resume your career.

While it is possible to obtain a job after being convicted of a felony, there are professions that you can't work in if you have a criminal record. For instance, if you were convicted of a felony, it's almost guaranteed that you can't be a police officer, work in a school as a teacher, or hold certain government positions. These are just a few of the

## FELONS AND EMPLOYMENT PRACTICES

As of 2012, the Equal Employment Opportunity Commission (EEOC), in conjunction with Title VII, enforced stricter guidelines in the practice of hiring convicted felons, ruling that disqualifying applicants with a criminal record could be considered discrimination.

industries in which a criminal background will largely affect your chances of being hired.

It is possible to have your record sealed, or expunged, but this is usually only possible for first-time offenders and for crimes that aren't considered to be too serious. Expungement varies by state, but general factors are the amount of time that has passed since the crime was committed, the severity of the crime, and the individual's overall criminal record. Additionally, the states of Arizona and New York do not allow the expungement of criminal records. If a judge decides that your record shouldn't be expunged, you'll be forced to carry around that criminal record for the rest of your life, which is something a lot of young people don't fully comprehend. This further proves that the decisions made at a young age can really affect your life as you grow older.

# RELATIONSHIPS WITH FAMILY AND FRIENDS

Being convicted of a felony can change the relationships that you have with your family and friends. Some people may not be understanding or forgiving of your actions, which is why relationships are sometimes strained when a person gets into legal trouble, especially if it's of a violent nature. It's important that you make a strong attempt to speak with your friends and family about the situation that you're in. They may want to hear your point of view or what drove you to commit a crime so that they can better understand the situation that you were in and how they can help you moving forward.

One important thing to know is that attorney-client privilege does not extend to friends and family. This means that they could be called to testify against you if they have

*Friends and family members can be a great source of support if you find yourself in legal trouble.*

knowledge that could get you convicted. Therefore, you should consult with your attorney about information that is safe to share with people close to you.

For relationships that may be strained because of your actions, it may take the assistance of a counselor to help you work through your differences with friends and family members. One of the most important things when trying to return to a normal life is having a support system, and it takes effort from both sides to achieve a healthy relationship.

## MEETING WITH YOUR PAROLE OFFICER

Whether you were initially put on probation as a punishment or served a prison sentence and are now on probation, meeting with a parole officer is a requirement. A parole officer, also known as a probation officer, is an individual appointed by the court system to monitor a person who has been punished by the law for committing a crime. The ultimate goal of the parole officer is to make sure that you're staying out of trouble, which could be done by scheduling weekly or monthly meetings.

Probation officers also have the liberty to search you or your property at any given time and require you to take a drug test. If you remain on good behavior and keep out of trouble, you may be able to get the judge to modify the terms of the probation, leading to a looser relationship between you and your parole officer. If you continue to show good behavior, your probationary period could be dropped altogether.

Violating your parole can lead to a slew of further legal troubles. Violating any terms of your parole can lead to it being revoked, meaning that a harsher penalty, like jail time, will result. The easiest way to avoid all of this is to show good behavior while on probation and prove to your parole officer that you are staying out of trouble. The better your behavior is while you are on probation, the sooner you can return to a normal life.

While returning to normalcy certainly extends further than returning to school or getting a job, they are the best ways to get back on your feet. Education is a gateway to a successful career, while employment is what helps a person make a living. Being convicted of a felony and spending time in prison can derail your life for a period of time, but it's important to know that you can come back from your conviction and make a successful life for yourself with perseverance and hard work.

# CHAPTER 5

# HOW TO AVOID BEING CONVICTED OF A VIOLENT FELONY

After learning what you have up to this point, one thing should become increasingly clear: being convicted of a felony is a serious offense and can turn your life completely upside down. That's not to say that you can't recover from it and eventually get back to your life, but wouldn't it just be easier to stay out of trouble and avoid being convicted of a felony altogether?

Something that a lot of people don't realize is that criminal activity is expensive for the country. According to the National School Board Association (NSBA), experts estimate that the United States saves anywhere from $1.7 to $2.3 million by preventing a high-risk youth from adopting a life of crime. There are a number of ways for juveniles to avoid the legal system and getting into trouble.

## HAVING A RELIABLE GROUP OF FRIENDS

One of the easiest ways to avoid getting into trouble is to have a good, supportive group of friends who look out for your safety and genuinely care about both your and their own futures. Since most teenagers spend a lot of time with their friends, it's important that their friends create a positive environment. It's not uncommon for juveniles to consider their friends as their own family, which makes having the right group of friends all the more important. Teens often caught up in the wrong crowd and end up making bad decisions based upon what their friends are doing.

So, how do you know if you're not hanging out with the right kind of people? Things like doing drugs, drinking alcohol, using violence, and skipping class immediately

*Drugs can lead to a lot of problems for teenagers. Avoid them, as well as friends who use them.*

come to mind as factors that should indicate that the crowd you're hanging out with is bound to lead to trouble. If you do find yourself caught up in the wrong group of friends, there are ways to meet new people and stay active, such as joining a sports team or an after school program. In fact, research shows that students who participate in after school activities are less likely to commit a violent felony.

## STAY BUSY AFTER SCHOOL!

According to a study by the NSBA, violent juvenile crime is most likely to occur between 3 and 6 PM. The study also found that freshmen boys who were left out of the Quantum Opportunity program, an after-school enrichment and incentives program for socioeconomically disadvantaged youth, were six times more likely to be convicted of a crime.

# SPORTS TEAMS AND AFTER SCHOOL PROGRAMS

Whether it's a sports team, a band, a club, or another form of after school program, filling your time with productive activities will cut back on the odds of getting into trouble, and worse, being arrested or convicted of a felony. Joining a sports team can be valuable, as it teaches important life skills, such as teamwork, sharing, commitment, and establishing goals. The same can be said for joining a club or being a member of a band. Just being a part of something can do wonders for anyone at a young age because it gives a sense of belonging.

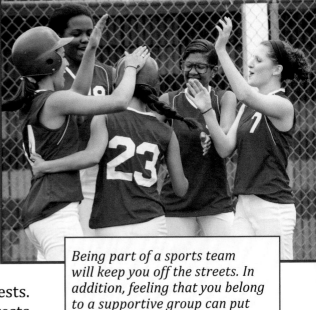

The same can be said for after school programs. Not only do after school programs help keep kids safe, but they also promote further learning and teach new skills and interests. These newfound interests could result in improved performance in school, thus

*Being part of a sports team will keep you off the streets. In addition, feeling that you belong to a supportive group can put you on the right path.*

leading to a better educational experience. Since a proper education is the foundation to a successful career, it's easy to see how important an after school program can be in regards to keeping juveniles away from trouble and on the right educational path.

## AVOIDING PEER PRESSURE AND RECIDIVISM

While everyone has the option to make choices for themselves, the fact is that not everyone does. Peer pressure is common among middle school and high school students, with individuals urging others to do things that a person may not originally want to do. When the pressure of their peers gets to be too much, some individuals will cave and start following other people instead of making decisions for themselves. For example, you may be pressured by your peers to rob a store, even though you may not want to. The pressure to be "cool" and fit in with a crowd is sometimes what leads a person to give in to peer pressure. If you're being pressured into doing something that you don't want to, it's important to stand up for yourself and do what you believe is right.

Even after being released from prison and serving your punishment, it's imperative that you align yourself with the right people who will help you stay out of trouble and work toward a positive life. It's a problem if you're hanging around the same people that helped you land behind bars when you finish serving your punishment. All too often, convicts get out of prison only to relapse and commit another crime; this is known as recidivism. The Pew Center of the State defines recidivism as "the act of reengaging in criminal offending despite having been punished." According to the National Criminal Justice Reference Service (NCJRS), there is no national recidivism rate for juveniles, but statistics are kept for adults. Per the Pew Center of the State's State of Recidivism report in 2011, the national three-year return-to-prison rate for individuals released in 2004 was 43.3 percent. That means that 43.3 percent of adults released from prison in 2004 found themselves right back behind bars in 2007.

# PROFESSIONAL ORGANIZATIONS

In addition to participating in an activity like a sport or club, there are professional organizations that aim to help juveniles with everything from drug and alcohol abuse to crime prevention. For example, the Big Brothers Big Sisters (BBBS) Community-Based Mentoring (CBM) Program is an organization that attempts to reduce risk factors for negative behavior in juveniles by providing positive adult contact and activities. Another form of help can come in the form of an Aggression Replacement Training (ART) program. The ART program is a ten-week, thirty-hour program that takes place three times a week with a group of eight to twelve juveniles. The goal of the program is to teach participants how to recognize and control their anger, which could have led them to commit a violent

*Residents of the Rosa Parks Center, a detention center for young girls, have a group discussion with their youth specialist. These group discussions attempt to reform teens.*

felony. These are just a couple of examples of organizations that can help. If this is something that you think you'd be interested in, you should research organizations in your area and reach out to them to learn more information.

## UNDERSTANDING THE LAW

One of the best things that you can do to avoid being convicted of a felony is to understand the law. Knowing what constitutes a felony and the severity of potential punishments for committing the crime are things that you should be aware of. Knowing the ins and outs of the legal system pertaining to felonies will help you avoid getting into trouble.

It all starts and ends with you. While there are a lot of organizations and people out there willing to help you get through your problems, you are the only person who can make it happen. The decisions that you make at this age are what will help set the tone for your life down the road. Align yourself with the right people in life—people who genuinely care about you and your well-being—and don't hesitate to ask someone for help should you feel that you need it. And if you do find yourself in trouble, use what you've learned in this book to arm yourself against mistakes that could have an impact on the rest of your life.

# GLOSSARY

**arraignment** A legal proceeding where a criminal is informed of the charges against him or her.

**assault** The act of purposely harming or threatening to harm an individual.

**consent** Granting permission.

**conviction** The finding of guilt.

**electronic monitoring** Also known as electronic tagging or house arrest, electronic monitoring is a form of surveillance punishment where an individual is required to wear a bracelet that tracks his location at all times. This can also be a condition of bail.

**expungement** The sealing or wiping of an individual's criminal record. It should be noted that certain entities such as law enforcement and government agencies can still see the record.

**felony** A crime, usually violent, that is punishable by at least one year in prison or the death penalty.

**grand jury** A group of jurors tasked with determining whether a case should go to trial.

**indictment** A formal charge.

**manslaughter** The unintentional killing of a human being by another human being.

**Miranda rights** A warning by the police before interrogation to ensure statements made are admissible in court.

**misdemeanor** A crime that isn't as serious as a felony and is punishable by a fine or up to one year in prison.

**parole** The early release of a prisoner prior to completing a prison sentence (sometimes because of to good behavior in prison).

**plea** A formal statement of guilt or innocence.

**plea bargain** An agreement in which a defendant pleads guilty to a charge in order to receive a deal from the prosecutor.

**preliminary hearing** A legal proceeding that takes place after a criminal complaint has been filed by the prosecutor to rule whether there's enough evidence against the defendant to warrant a trial.

**probation** A punishment handed down by the court where an individual who has been found guilty avoids jail time but is under the supervision of a probation officer.

**prosecutor** An attorney whose job it is to convict a defendant.

**rape** Sexual intercourse or activity without consent.

**recidivism** When a person who had previously served time for committing a crime returns to prison for committing another crime.

**robbery** The use of violence or the threat of physical harm to steal someone else's property.

**trial** A legal proceeding to determine if a defendant is guilty of a crime.

The Campaign for Youth Justice
1220 L Street NW, Suite 605
Washington, DC 20005
(202) 558-3580
Website: http://www.campaignforyouthjustice.org
The Campaign for Youth Justice is a member organization
whose goal is to end the trying, sentencing, and incar-
cerating of juveniles (youth under the age of eighteen)
in the adult criminal justice system.

Canada's Economic Action Plan
Service Canada
Ottawa, Ontario K1A 0J9
Canada
(800) 622-6232
Website: http://actionplan.gc.ca/en
Among many other things, the mission of Canada's Economic
Action Plan is to prevent youth crime and provide ser-
vices for juveniles who get in trouble with the law.

The Center for Children's Law and Policy
1701 K Street NW, Suite 1100
Washington, DC 20006
(202) 637-0377
Website: http://www.cclp.org
The Center for Children's Law and Policy is a public interest
organization that works to reduce the unnecessary
imprisonment of juveniles without jeopardizing the
public and improve the conditions of the facilities
where juveniles are held during imprisonment.

The Coalition for Juvenile Justice
1319 F Street NW, Suite 402
Washington, DC 20004
(202) 467-0864
Website: http://www.juvjustice.org
The Coalition for Juvenile Justice aims to prevent children
and youth from getting involved in the court system
and help children who have been charged receive the
best care in the juvenile court system.

Juvenile Law Center
The Philadelphia Building
1315 Walnut Street, 4th Floor
Philadelphia, PA 19107
(800) 875-8887
Website: http://jlc.org
The Juvenile Law Center is the oldest nonprofit law firm for
juveniles in the country and focuses on child welfare in
the justice system.

Newcomers Employment and Education Development
Services (NEEDS Inc.)
251-A Notre Dame Avenue
Winnipeg, Manitoba R3B 1N8
Canada
(204) 940-1260
Website: http://www.needsinc.ca
NEEDS Inc. supports the integration of refugee juveniles
into Canadian life and aids to prevent them from
engaging in criminal activity.

Office of Juvenile Justice and Delinquency Prevention
810 Seventh Street NW
Washington, DC 20531
(202) 307–5911
Website: http://www.ojjdp.gov
The Office of Juvenile Justice and Delinquency Prevention's
  purpose is to implement programs for juveniles that
  will keep them away from crime and other delinquent
  activities.

## WEBSITES

Because of the changing nature of Internet links, Rosen Publishing has developed an online list of websites related to the subject of this book. This site is updated regularly. Please use this link to access this list:

http://www.rosenlinks.com/KYR/Felo

# FOR FURTHER READING

Gerdes, Louise I., ed. *Juvenile Crime* (Opposing Viewpoints). Detroit, MI: Greenhaven Press, 2012.

Haerens, Margaret, ed. *Juvenile Crime* (Global Viewpoints). Detroit, MI: Greenhaven Press, 2013.

Haugen, David M., and Susan Musser, eds. *Juvenile Justice* (Teen Rights and Freedoms). Detroit, MI: Greenhaven Press, 2013.

Hile, Lori. *Gangs* (Teen Issues). Chicago, IL: Heinemann Library, 2012.

Hinds, Maurene J. *You Have the Right to Know Your Rights*. Berkeley Heights, NJ: Enslow Publishers, 2005.

Lassieur, Allison. *Violent Crime* (Hot Topics). Chicago, IL: Heinemann Library, 2011.

Merino, Noel, ed. *Juvenile Crime* (Introducing Issues with Opposing Viewpoints). Farmington Hills, MI: Greenhaven Press, 2010.

Taylor, Robert, and Eric Fritsch. *Juvenile Justice: Policies, Programs, and Practices*. New York, NY: McGraw-Hill, 2010.

Truly, Traci. *Teen Rights (and Responsibilities): A Legal Guide for Teens and the Adults in Their Lives*. Naperville, IL: Sphinx Publishers, 2005.

Vander Hook, Sue. *Miranda v. Arizona*. Minneapolis, MN: Abdo, 2012.

Williams, Heidi. *Juvenile Crime (Issues that Concern You)*. Farmington Hills, MI: Greenhaven Press, 2010.

# BIBLIOGRAPHY

Annie E. Casey Foundation. "Kids Count Data Snapshot: Youth Incarceration In the United States." Retrieved January 29, 2014 (http://www.aecf.orgKnowledgeCenter/Public ationsaspx?pubguid=%7BDFAD838E-1C29-46B4-BE8A-4D8392BC25C9%7D).

Belli, Melvin, and A. Wilkinson. *Everybody's Guide to the Law*. New York, NY: Harcourt Brace Jovanovich, Publishers, 1986.

Bergman, Paul. "Assault, Battery, and Aggravated Assault." Nolo.com. Retrieved February 11, 2014 (http://www.nolo.com/legal-encyclopedia/assault-battery-aggra-vated-assault-33775.html).

Berman, Sara. "Living With Your Probation." Nolo.com. Retrieved February 11, 2014 (http://www.nolo.com/legal-encyclopedia/living-with-your-probation.html).

Berman, Sara. "Paying a Private Criminal Defense Attorney." Nolo.com. Retrieved February 11, 2014 (http://www.nolo.com/legal-encyclopedia/paying-private-crimi-nal-defense-attorney.html).

Big Brothers Big Sisters. "Community-Based Programs." Retrieved February 19, 2014 (http://www.bbbs.org/site/c.9iILI3NGKhK6F/b.5960985/k.6676/CommunityBased_Programs.htm).

Center for Employment Opportunities in New York. Retrieved January 21, 2014. (http://ceoworks.org).

Children's Defense Fund. "Juvenile Justice." Retrieved February 1, 2014 (http://www.childrensdefense.org/policy-priorities/juvenile-justice).

CNN. "Death Penalty Fast Facts." Retrieved February 15, 2014 (http://www.cnn.com/2013/07/19/us death-penalty-fast-facts).

Cornell University Law School. "Assault and Battery." Retrieved February 24, 2014 (http://www.law.cornell.edu/wex/assault_and_battery).

Federal Bureau of Investigation (FBI). "Crime in the United States, 2012." Retrieved January 7, 2014 (http://www.fbi.gov/news/stories/2013/september/latest-crime-stats-  released/latest-crime-stats-released).

Federal Bureau of Investigation (FBI). "Gangs." Retrieved on January 22, 2014 (http://www.fbi.gov/about-us/investigate/vc_majorthefts/gangs).

Federal Bureau of Investigation (FBI). "2011 National Gang Threat Assessment—Emerging Trends." Retrieved January 7, 2014 (http://www.fbi.gov/stats-services/publications/2011-national-gang-threat-assessment).

Federal Bureau of Investigation (FBI). "Violent Crime." Retrieved January 7, 2014 (http://www.fbi.gov/about-us/cjis/ucr/crime-in-the-u.s/2011/crime-in-the-u.s.-2011/violent-crime/violent-crime).

Federal Bureau of Prisons. "Custody and Care." Retrieved May 13, 2014 (http://www.bop.gov/inmates/custody_and_care/substance_abuse_treatment.jsp).

Fettig, Amy, and Tanya Greene. "Time Out is For Kids. This Isn't." American Civil Liberties Union. Retrieved January 2, 2014 (https://www.aclu.org/blog/prisoners-rights-criminal-law-reform/time-out-kids-isnt).

Goudie & Kohn, P.A. "Federal and State Crimes." Retrieved January 22, 2014 (http://www.goudiekohn.com/practice-areas/federal-state-crime/).

Guerin, Lisa. "Getting Hired with an Arrest or Conviction Record." Nolo.com. Retrieved February 6, 2014

(http://www.nolo.com/legal-encyclopedia/getting-hired-with-arrest-conviction-record.html).

Hansen, Louis. "Life Times Six: Do the Crime, Do the Time." The Virginian-Pilot. Retrieved January 6, 2014 (http://hamptonroads.com/2013/11/life-times-six-part-2-do-crime-do-time#interactive).

Howell, John. *Everyday Law for Everyone.* Blue Ridge Summit, PA: Liberty House, 1987.

Michon, Kathleen. "Juvenile Court Sentencing Options." Nolo.com. Retrieved February 24, 2014 (http://www.nolo.com/legal-encyclopedia/juvenile-court-sentenc-ing-options-32225.html).

National Criminal Justice Reference Service (NCJRS). "What is the National Juvenile Recidivism Rate?" Retrieved February 19, 2014 (https://www.ncjrs.gov/app/QA/Detail.aspx?Id=113&context=9).

National Institute of Justice. "Aggression Replacement Training (ART)." Retrieved January 4, 2014 (http://www.crimesolutions.gov/ProgramDetails.aspx?ID=254).

National Institute of Justice. "Juveniles." Retrieved January 4, 2014 (http://www.crimesolutions.gov/TopicDetails.aspx?ID=5).

National Institute of Justice. "Shock Incarceration in New York." Retrieved May 13, 2014 (https://www.ncjrs.gov/pdffiles/shockny.pdf).

Newman, Sanford, James Fox, Edward Flynn, and William Christenson. "America's After-School Choice: The Prime Time for Juvenile Crime,Or Youth Enrichment and Achievement." National School Boards Association. Retrieved February 14, 2014 (http://www.nsba.org/

Board-Leadership/EDLO/WhatIsExtendedDay/
AmericasAfterSchoolChoice.pdf).

OJJDP. "Statistical Briefing Book." Online. Retrieved May
13, 2014. (http://www.ojjdp.gov/ojstatbb/crime/
JAR_Display.asp?ID=qa05200)

Opell, Richard. "Ohio Teenagers Guilty in Rape That Social
Media Brought to Light." New York Times, 2013.
Retrieved January 22, 2014. (http://www.nytimes.
com/2013/03/18/us/teenagers-found-guilty-in-rape-
in-steubenville-ohio.html?pagewanted=all&_r=2&).

Pew Center on the States. "State of Recidivism:
The Revolving Door of America's Prisons."
Retrieved February 20, 2014 (http://www.
pewtrusts.org/uploadedFiles/wwwpewtrustsorg/
Reports /sentencing_and_corrections/ State_Recid
ivism_Revolving_Door_America_Prisons%20.pdf).

Stamm, Alex. "15-Year-Old Gets Six Life Sentences?"
American Civil Liberties Union. Retrieved
December 20, 2013 (https://www.aclu.org/blog/
criminal-law-reform-human-rights/15-year-old-gets-
six-life-sentences).

Tarleton, Michael. "Pleading Guilty While Saying You're
Innocent." Nolo.com. Retrieved February 11, 2014
(http://www.nolo.com/legal-encyclopedia/pleading-
guilty-while-saying-youre-innocent.html).

University of Central Florida Police Department. "Crime
Definitions." Retrieved January 4, 2014 (http://police.
ucf.edu/CSAstyles/Crime%20Definitions.pdf).

U.S. Department of Labor. "Bureau of Labor Statistics."
Retrieved February 14, 2014 (http://research.stlouis-
fed.org/fred2/series/HS4N25OW).

U.S. Equal Employment Opportunity Commission. "EEOC Endorsement Guidance." Retrieved January 21, 2014 (http://www.eeoc.gov/laws/guidance/arrest_conviction.cfm).

Wright, James. "Tommy Wells' 'Ban the Box' Bill Gets Strong Support." The Washington Informer. Retrieved February 11, 2014 (http://washingtoninformer.com/news/2014/feb/10/tommy-wells-ban-the-box-bill-gets-strong-support).

Yale School of Forestry & Environmental Studies. "Urban Resources Initiative." Retrieved February 2, 2014 (http://environment.yale.edu/uri).

# INDEX

## ABOUT THE AUTHOR

Pete Schauer is a writer from Brick, New Jersey. He holds an M.A. from William Paterson University in professional communication and currently works for a digital marketing and web development agency. When he's not writing, Schauer enjoys sports and spending time with his fiancée.

## ABOUT THE EXPERT REVIEWER

Lindsay A. Lewis, Esq., is a practicing criminal defense attorney in New York City, where she handles a wide range of matters, from those discussed in this series to high-profile federal criminal cases. She believes that each and every defendant deserves a vigorous and informed defense. Ms. Lewis is a graduate of the Benjamin N. Cardozo School of Law and Vassar College.

## PHOTO CREDITS

Cover © iStockphoto.com/ariusz; cover background Christophe Rolland/Shutterstock.com; pp. 4–5 Photofusion/Universal Images Group/Getty Images; p. 9 AFP/Getty Images; pp. 12, 31, 49 © AP Images; p. 14 Jose Cabezas/AFP/Getty Images; p. 17 Trista Weibel-l/E+/Getty Images; p. 20 Miami Herald/McClatchy-Tribune/Getty Images; p. 22 Ron Chapple/The Image Bank/Getty Images; p. 27 The Washington Post/Getty Images; p. 29 Spencer Grant/age fotostock; p. 33 John Moore/Getty Images; pp. 36–37 Image Source/Digital Vision/Getty Images; p. 39 Bloomberg/Getty Images; p. 41 KidStock/Blend Images/Getty Images; p. 45 sturti/E+/Getty Images; p. 47 Yellow Dog Productions/Iconica/Getty Images.

Designer: Brian Garvey; Editor: Christine Poolos